W9-BDG-456

WEST VIRGINIA

EXPLORE THE UNITED STATES

Sarah Tieck

Big Buddy BOOKS

Explore the United States

Published by ABDO Publishing Company, PO Box 398166, Minneapolis, MN 55439.

Printed in the United States of America, North Mankato, Minnesota.
062012
092012

 PRINTED ON RECYCLED PAPER

Coordinating Series Editor: Rochelle Baltzer
Contributing Editors: Megan M. Gunderson, Marcia Zappa
Graphic Design: Adam Craven
Cover Photograph: *Shutterstock*: Amanda Haddox.
Interior Photographs/Illustrations: *Alamy*: Everett Collection Inc (p. 13), Andre Jenny (p. 27), Mark Summerfield (p. 30); *AP Photo*: AP Photo (p. 25), Library of Congress (p. 23), North Wind Picture Archives via AP Images (p. 23); *Getty Images*: Michael P Gadomski/Photo Researchers (p. 17), Raymond Gehman/National Geographic (p. 21), Harrison Shull (p. 26); *iStockphoto*: ©iStockphoto.com/appelletr (p. 27), ©iStockphoto.com/jodijacobson (pp. 9, 19), ©iStockphoto.com/matejphoto (p. 11), ©iStockphoto.com/Ogphoto (p. 5), ©iStockphoto.com/DenisTangneyJr (p. 11); *Shutterstock*: Steve Byland (p. 30), Melinda Fawver (p. 30), Steve Heap (p. 27), Philip Lange (p. 30), Mary Terriberry (p. 29), zcw (p. 26).

All population figures taken from the 2010 US census.

Library of Congress Cataloging-in-Publication Data

Tieck, Sarah, 1976-
  West Virginia / Sarah Tieck.
     p. cm. -- (Explore the United States)
  ISBN 978-1-61783-388-5
  1. West Virginia--Juvenile literature. I. Title.
  F241.3.T49 2013
  975.4--dc23
                                    2012018236

6698

Contents

One Nation

The United States is a **diverse** country. It has farmland, cities, coasts, and mountains. Its people come from many different backgrounds. And, its history covers more than 200 years.

Today the country includes 50 states. West Virginia is one of these states. Let's learn more about this state and its story!

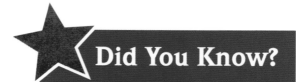

Did You Know?

West Virginia became a state on June 20, 1863. It was the thirty-fifth state to join the nation.

West Virginia is known for its hills and mountains.

WEST VIRGINIA UP CLOSE

The United States has four main **regions**. West Virginia is in the South.

West Virginia has five states on its borders. Pennsylvania and Maryland are northeast. Virginia is east and south. Kentucky is southwest. Ohio is northwest.

West Virginia has a total area of 24,230 square miles (62,755 sq km). About 1.9 million people live there.

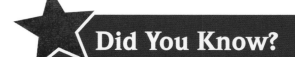

Did You Know?

Washington DC is the US capital city. Puerto Rico is a US commonwealth. This means it is governed by its own people.

REGIONS OF THE UNITED STATES

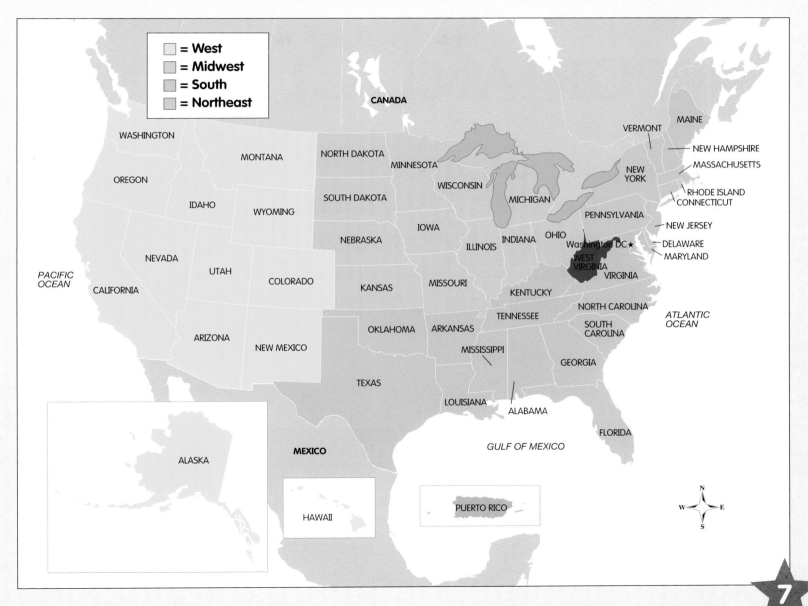

Legend:
- = West
- = Midwest
- = South
- = Northeast

CANADA

WASHINGTON
MONTANA
NORTH DAKOTA
MINNESOTA
OREGON
IDAHO
WYOMING
SOUTH DAKOTA
WISCONSIN
MICHIGAN
NEW YORK
VERMONT
MAINE
NEW HAMPSHIRE
MASSACHUSETTS
RHODE ISLAND
CONNECTICUT
IOWA
NEBRASKA
ILLINOIS
INDIANA
OHIO
PENNSYLVANIA
NEW JERSEY
DELAWARE
MARYLAND
NEVADA
UTAH
COLORADO
KANSAS
MISSOURI
Washington DC ★
WEST VIRGINIA
VIRGINIA
PACIFIC OCEAN
CALIFORNIA
KENTUCKY
NORTH CAROLINA
ATLANTIC OCEAN
ARIZONA
NEW MEXICO
OKLAHOMA
ARKANSAS
TENNESSEE
SOUTH CAROLINA
MISSISSIPPI
GEORGIA
TEXAS
LOUISIANA
ALABAMA
FLORIDA
ALASKA
MEXICO
GULF OF MEXICO
HAWAII
PUERTO RICO

N
W E
S

7

IMPORTANT CITIES

West Virginia's **capital** is Charleston. It is also the state's largest city, with 51,400 people.

Charleston is located where the Kanawha and Elk Rivers meet. It has been the state capital since 1885. It was also the capital from 1870 to 1875.

Did You Know?

Wheeling was West Virginia's first capital.

West Virginia

Parkersburg

Huntington
★Charleston

West Virginia's state capitol has a golden dome.

Huntington is West Virginia's second-largest city. It is home to 49,138 people. This port city is located along the Ohio River. Many products made in Huntington are shipped on the river.

Parkersburg is the state's third-largest city. It is home to 31,492 people. It is located where the Ohio and Little Kanawha Rivers meet.

Huntington is the center of a large business area that includes parts of Ohio and Kentucky.

Parkersburg got its name in 1811. It honors one of the area's first settlers.

WEST VIRGINIA IN HISTORY

West Virginia's history includes Native Americans, colonists, and war. Native Americans were the first to live in present-day West Virginia.

Europeans began settling the area in the 1700s. At that time, West Virginia was part of the Virginia Colony.

In 1788, the land was part of the new state of Virginia. In 1861, the country was split by the **American Civil War**. At this time, West Virginia separated from Virginia to support the North. It became its own state in 1863.

On October 16, 1859, John Brown led a raid in Harpers Ferry. This action brought attention to the country's slavery problem.

Timeline

1859

John Brown led a group of people who were against **slavery** in a raid. They tried to take weapons from the US military in Harpers Ferry.

1863

West Virginia became the thirty-fifth state.

1800s

The western part of Virginia said it would not support the Southern states during the **American Civil War**. This area made its own government to support the North.

1861

Two mines exploded in Monongah. The blasts killed 362 people. This was the worst mine accident in US history.

1907

14

1954

The West Virginia Turnpike opened. This road connected the cities of Charleston and Princeton.

1972

The Buffalo Creek Flood was one of the worst in West Virginia's history. More than 100 people died.

2010

Despite better safety laws over the years, 29 miners died when a mine exploded.

1900s

2000s

A mine explosion killed 78 miners. This led to new safety laws in the United States.

1968

Mary Lou Retton of Fairmont took part in the Summer Olympics. She became the first American female to win a gold medal in all-around gymnastics.

1984

ACROSS THE LAND

West Virginia is known for its mountains. The Blue Ridge and Allegheny (a-luh-GAY-nee) Mountains are in the east. The state also has hills, valleys, forests, and rivers. Major rivers include the Ohio, the Kanawha, and the Monongahela.

Many types of animals make their homes in this state. These include bears, deer, foxes, raccoons, and bass.

Did You Know?

In July, the average temperature in West Virginia is 72°F (22°C). In January, it is 32°F (0°C).

Spruce Knob is in the Allegheny Mountains. It is West Virginia's highest point, at 4,861 feet (1,482 m).

17

Earning a Living

West Virginia is known for its natural **resources**. Coal is a major product of the state's mines. Farmers produce livestock, apples, and hay.

West Virginia has many other important businesses. Most people work in service jobs, such as helping visitors to the state or working for the government. Others work in factories that make **chemicals**, metal products, glass, and foods.

West Virginia has been known for coal mining since the late 1800s.

Natural Wonder

Monongahela National Forest is in eastern West Virginia. It includes mountains, valleys, rivers, and streams.

Some say the forest's name comes from a Native American word. It means "falling banks." People visit the forest to hike, bike, camp, fish, and ride horses.

Monongahela National Forest is one of the largest hardwood forests in the eastern United States.

HOMETOWN HEROES

Many famous people have lived in West Virginia. Booker T. Washington was born to **slaves** in Virginia in 1856. When his parents were freed, the family moved to Malden.

Washington became known for helping make life better for African Americans. He worked as a teacher. In 1881, he started a school for African Americans in Tuskegee, Alabama. This is now known as Tuskegee University.

Washington's birthplace in Virginia is open to visitors.

Washington wrote a book called *Up from Slavery* about his life.

23

Pearl S. Buck was born in Hillsboro in 1892. She grew up in China and became a famous author.

The Good Earth is Buck's most well-known book. It is about a Chinese farmer. This book helped people learn more about life in China.

Buck won the 1932 Pulitzer Prize for *The Good Earth*.

Tour Book

Do you want to go to West Virginia? If you visit the state, here are some places to go and things to do!

 Taste

Take a big bite of a Golden Delicious apple. This type of apple was first grown in West Virginia.

 See

Watch rock climbers at Seneca Rocks. This popular landmark is in the Monongahela National Forest.

★ Remember

Visit Harpers Ferry National Historical Park. Learn about John Brown and this area's history.

★ Ride

Go white-water rafting! This is a popular activity in the state's parks and wild lands.

★ Discover

Ride the tram at Pipestem Resort State Park. It takes six minutes to ride down into the Bluestone River Gorge.

A Great State

The story of West Virginia is important to the United States. The people and places that make up this state offer something special to the country. Together with all the states, West Virginia helps make the United States great.

Blackwater Falls is just one of the state's natural wonders.

Fast Facts

Date of Statehood:
June 20, 1863

Population (rank):
1,852,994
(37th most-populated state)

Total Area (rank):
24,230 square miles
(41st largest state)

Motto:
"Montani Semper Liberi"
(Mountaineers Are Always
Free)

Nickname:
Mountain State

State Capital:
Charleston

Flag:

Flower: Rhododendron

Postal Abbreviation:
WV

Tree: Sugar Maple

Bird: Northern Cardinal

30

Important Words

American Civil War the war between the Northern and Southern states from 1861 to 1865.

capital a city where government leaders meet.

chemical (KEH-mih-kuhl) a substance that can cause reactions and changes.

diverse made up of things that are different from each other.

region a large part of a country that is different from other parts.

resource a supply of something useful or valued.

slavery the practice of owning people as slaves. A slave is a person who is bought and sold as property.

Web Sites

To learn more about West Virginia, visit ABDO Publishing Company online. Web sites about West Virginia are featured on our Book Links page. These links are routinely monitored and updated to provide the most current information available.

www.abdopublishing.com

Index